What On Earth Can It Be?

Roger McGough

Illustrated by Lydia Monks

PUFFIN BOOKS

What on earth can it be?

A piece of
starry-gazy pie?

A wizard's hat?

A circus ringmaster's
megaphone?

What on earth can it be?

It's a crocogiant
Having a midnight snack.
When he's had a tummy full
I hope he'll not come back.

What on earth can it be?

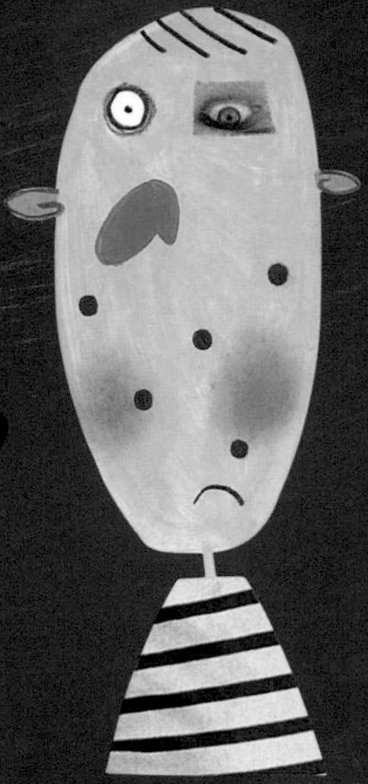

A nasty rash?

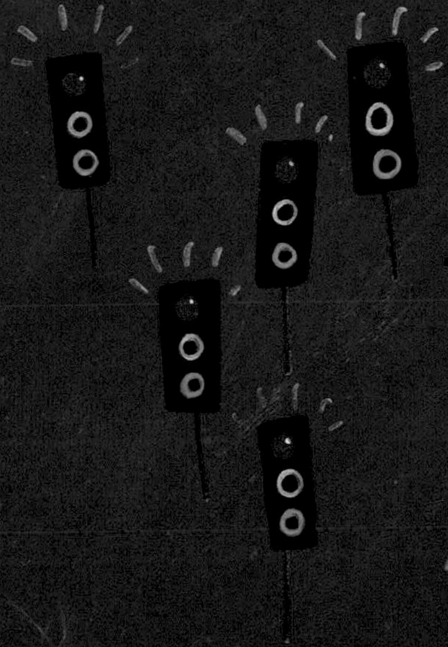

Traffic lights (all saying Don't Go)?

Five cherry drops (four for me
and one for you)?

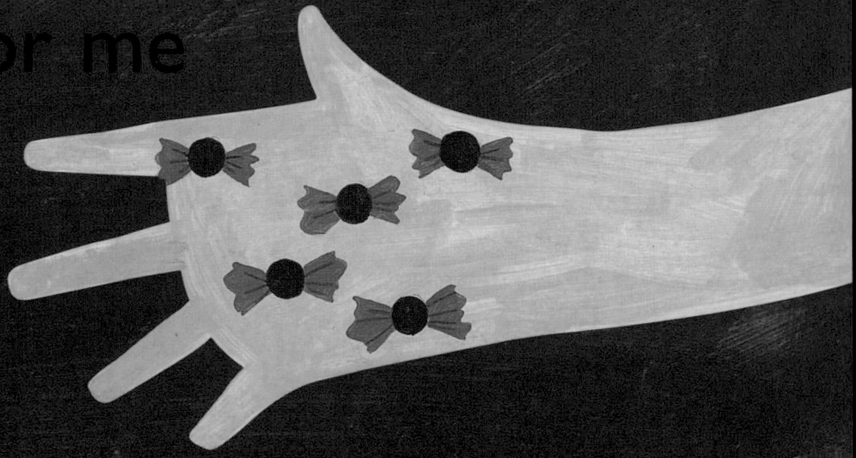

What on earth can it be?

It's a chuckle of clowns
Up to their tricks.
If you wanted to join them
There would be six.

What on earth can it be?

Unlucky throw?
Down you go.

A robot (feeling poorly)?

A piece of mouldy cheese?

What on earth can it be?

It's the moon
In search of the sky.
He's late for work
(Don't ask me why).

What on earth can it be?

Peg-legged pirates, walking the plank?

A ladder lying in the snow?

A piano keyboard, bored?

What on earth can it be?

It's a zebra

Sporting a scarf.

(It's polka-dotted.

Did you spot it?)

What on earth can it be?

A rocket? (Is there life in space?)

A truck travelling at speed?

A block to
build with and
help you read?

What on earth can it be?

The E D
el extremo
le fin

The END
of course!

Goodbye!